CAN YOU **LOVE** PASSED THE PAIN?

Can You Love Passed the Pain?

Anita Johnson

XULON ELITE

Xulon Press Elite
2301 Lucien Way #415
Maitland, FL 32751
407.339.4217
www.xulonpress.com

© 2022 by Anita Johnson

All rights reserved solely by the author. The author guarantees all contents are original and do not infringe upon the legal rights of any other person or work. No part of this book may be reproduced in any form without the permission of the author. The views expressed in this book are not necessarily those of the publisher.

Due to the changing nature of the Internet, if there are any web addresses, links, or URLs included in this manuscript, these may have been altered and may no longer be accessible. The views and opinions shared in this book belong solely to the author and do not necessarily reflect those of the publisher. The publisher, therefore, disclaims responsibility for the views or opinions expressed within the work.

Unless otherwise indicated, Scripture quotations taken from the King James Version (KJV)–*public domain*.

Paperback ISBN-13: 978-1-66286-250-2
Hard Cover ISBN-13: 978-1-66286-251-9
Ebook ISBN-13: 978-1-66286-252-6

Table of Contents

Chapter 1: Signs Before the Storm 1

Chapter 2: Walking on Eggshells 5

Chapter 3: A Wolf in Sheep's Clothing. 9

Chapter 4: I Totally Understand Your Pain. 13

Chapter 5: Feeling Alone: Don't Be Afraid to Ask for Help 19

Chapter 6: God Gave Me a Voice: This Is My Season. 23

CHAPTER 1

Signs Before the Storm

Have you ever noticed that before there is a storm, things change? The air changes, the clouds change, even some animals act differently. The meteorologist will let you know what to expect, how to dress, and when to take shelter.

Now, we all don't have a personal meteorologist when it comes to relationships. There's not always someone there who can tell us what is going to happen before it happens. Our animals don't always run away, the air doesn't feel thicker, but when an abuser enters our lives, there are always warning signs. If you're honest, there may have been signs that you just didn't see. God has a way of warning you when a person is not right for you. He did for me.

The first time He warned me was when I had just met my abuser. I could see the red flags all around him, but I ignored the warning signs. It's like seeing the flags at the beach, saying, "Beware of the sharks." When you go in anyway, you can't blame the shark for biting you.

I remember the first time God gave me a way out. Yes, there were many times God rescued me. I was so relieved. I was praising God, thanking Him for saving me from him, vowing never to go back again. You must be so careful; my abuser was very charming, promising that he had gotten help and would not hit me again. He would tell me that he loved me, then he would say, "But if you wouldn't do things to make me hit you." He would always blame me for the abuse.

Sometimes, when we are in an abusive or toxic relationship, we can mistake lust for love. The title of this book is *Can you **love** passed the pain?* God never wants us to lust after things. That is why He said to have no other God before Him, because He knew that you couldn't love God *and* the Devil. You would lust after one and love the other.

Lust is an emotion that can get you into so much trouble. Why do you think God tells us not to lust? In 1 Peter 2:11 (KJV), we read, "Dearly beloved, I beseech you as strangers and pilgrims, abstain from fleshly lusts, which war against the soul." When you are lusting, you are warring against your very own soul; you are not going after what God want you to do but after things that are not for us. The definition of lust is having a very strong desire for someone or something. Lust will cause you to go after the wrong thing and not listen to what God is trying to say to you. I was lusting after my abuser, and it caused me not to listen to God and then I felt like God no longer heard me. I felt all alone, which caused me to make some bad choices. James 1:14 (KJV) says, "But every man is tempted, when he is drawn away of his own lust and enticed."

I was so very closed minded, and my eyes were closed to what I was reading in God's Word. I didn't love this man, but I know now that I lusted after him. It was not a sexual thing; it was a strong desire to have a man in my life.

In October of 2010, you see, I had just found out that my husband of twenty years had cheated, and the woman he was leaving me for was pregnant. I thought I had something special because I was the only woman that had kids by him, and now there was another woman. I was heartbroken and very upset, so I turned to my abuser, thinking he would make everything alright, not even thinking about God as being the one I should have turned to.

Like I said from the beginning, the warning signs were there. He was very controlling. He didn't really want me to be away from him, but

I wanted to be with someone because I thought that would make the pain go away. My abuser seemed like the answer to my dreams at the time. He acted like he loved my kids; he would cook for us because he was a chef. He would have food ready for us, and all I had to do was pick it up. Him doing these sweet things was just the calm before the storm. As I said before, in a toxic/abusive relationship, there are signs that a storm is brewing. Here are some of these signs (and there are more).

SIGNS BEFORE THE STORM

1. You are frightened by your partner's temper.
2. You are afraid to disagree with your partner.
3. You have been hit, kicked, or shoved by your partner.
4. You don't see your friends or family.
5. You have been forced to have sex or have been afraid to say no to sex.
6. You have been forced to explain everything that you do, every place you go, and every person that you see to avoid your partner's temper.
7. You believe that you can't live without your partner or that you can't get enough of your partner.
8. You believe that marriage will change your partner. (Believe it or not, the abuse did not just start when you got married; it started before that.)
9. Your partner makes you feel worse about yourself.
10. You have fewer and fewer happy times together, and more and more of your time is spent on apologies, promises, anger, guilt, and fear.

www.google.com/abuse

Never be ashamed of a scar it simply means you were stronger than whatever tried to hurt you.

— Author unknown

Chapter 2

Walking on Eggshells

Your abuser has many sides. One day, your abuser is up and happy. You are the joy of their life, and you can't do anything wrong in their eyes. Your abuser is praising you to family and friends. You are on cloud nine, just loving the relationship, but in your mind, you are waiting for the next shoe to drop.

In public, maybe you are making sure you don't do anything to upset them. You make sure that if another person looks your way, you are looking in another direction so your abuser doesn't feel like you are looking at the person that is looking at you.

Maybe your abuser calls you, and you pray that the phone call goes through and doesn't drop because if it does, your abuser will say you hung up on them and were cheating or with another person. The abuse happens again, and you start walking on eggshells to make sure you don't make them upset.

Domestic violence is a cycle, like riding on a roller coast or a merry-go-round: It will continue until someone decides to get off, beginning with stage one.

Stage 1: Transition Building

> You feel as though you are walking on eggshells or waiting for the other shoe to drop. Your abuser is edgy,

moody, easily agitated, and unpredictable. There is an air of heightened anxiety.

Stage 2: Abuse or Abusive

This is the most violent stage, characterized by concentrated, intense emotional and verbal abuse, physical abuse, and the explosion or eruption of the tension previously described. It is in this stage where most people realize there may be something wrong, but they are too afraid to do anything. Stage three is why victims don't leave. Why? They feel like their abuser will change "this time." They feel like their abuser truly loves them, or they stay because of the kids, or (here is a big one) they feel like they are a failure in their marriage if they leave.

Stage 3: Honeymoon

He/she says, "I'm sorry," and "I'll never do it again." Your abuser may blame you for their actions, saying things like "If you wouldn't act like that …" or "If you wouldn't disappear when you leave the house, I wouldn't get angry." Your abuser may try to make up with cards, candy, flowers, or sex. They experience many feelings from anger to love to confusion. You believe your abuser, and the cycle continues.

www.domesticviolencestages.com

Love yourself enough to save yourself from yourself. Jump off the roller coaster. It is okay to be by yourself; it is there where you learn who you are. Love yourself enough to be with yourself, or rekindle the relationship you had with family and friends.

Sometimes, burning bridges isn't a bad thing. It prevents you from going back to a place, you should never have been in the first place.

www.picturesquotes.com

Chapter 3

A Wolf in Sheep's Clothing

Now, let me share with you a little about my story, as it may help you in your journey. My abuser was a wolf in sheep's clothing. He would wine and dine me, buy me flowers and candies, and open the door for me. I didn't want for anything. Everything a woman could ask for, my abuser was it. So, I looked over the warning signs, like him being controlling, wanting to know where I was every moment of the day. I just thought he loved me and wanted to be very protective over me.

I would sometimes tell myself, *"This is too good to be true,"* and I found out it was. He had some of my family fooled too. They loved him because they never saw the abuse, and I was so good at hiding it. They thought he had rescued me from the horrible drama that I was going through with my first husband.

I met my abuser when I was going through the worst time in my life. As I mentioned before, I was in a very bad place. My husband of twenty years had walked out on me and the kids and was living with the other woman. He had gotten her pregnant and then to top it all off, he was in the military, so we were in a military town. He had a lot of pull in the town, and he took everything from me; my home, my vehicle, my children. I was left homeless and alone. He divorced me and he married her.

My relationship with my abuser was the only thing I thought I had. I had moved so far away from God that I thought He didn't know me or didn't hear me anymore. My abuser was right there, whispering in my ear that *he* had me and I didn't need my family or friends anymore. He assured me that *he* was God-sent, and I believed him. I felt like the luckiest woman in the world, and I ignored the warnings—even from my kids. I just thought they wanted me back with their father.

The first time he lost his temper, I thought it was cute because he was jealous of me talking with a childhood friend. I assured him that he was just a friend, and I would stop talking to him if he liked and that I loved him and only him. He would always call me his "queen," and he wanted me to call him my "king." He would go to church with me, so I thought, "*Maybe he* is *right for me.*" My kids didn't think so. They started acting out. The teenagers were leaving the house and not coming back in time for curfew. Even the young kids didn't want me to leave the house with him, but I still ignored the warnings.

My ex-husband had moved on with the other woman, and he moved her to the same city I was in. I decided that was enough. I couldn't take seeing them out together and being a happy little family when I was suffering and my family had been taken away from me. At this time, my ex would still come over and try to control my life. He would try to tell me when I should go out, who I should see, and he was even trying to tell me that I should sleep with him and no one else. He told me that I was only supposed to be with him, but he had a whole other family on the other side of town. I decided I was going to get away for a little while. I left to live with my family in Georgia, but the mistake I made was taking my abuser with me.

Everything was going well until I started spending time with my family and going out more. He would call me all the time when I was out with my sister. I would go to church, and he would call and want me to answer the phone while I was in church. I had to check in everywhere I went. I was so getting tired of him, but he was the only one that had a job and was paying the bills.

When I didn't get back in touch with him on time or when he wanted me to, then he would threaten to kill himself because "I didn't love him," and "I took him away from his children that loved him." It was always my fault. Like I said, many signs were there, but I was not paying attention. I just thought he was acting that way because he loved me.

I really wanted to get away from him at this point, but he had a hold on me. I thought I couldn't make it without him. My ex had gone to court and took my kids because I was homeless. My abuser told me he was the only way that I could get my kids back. I had really forgotten about God even though I was going to church. I was still trying to praise God, but I was hurting too. I had never felt this way before. My kids were gone, and my abuser was in control of me. But God never left me. He was always there. He would give me a way out, but I was scared to take it. I almost got the nerve to send my abuser back to Virginia, but he told me I would not make it without him, and I fell for it.

Now, I know you are wondering, "Why didn't she just leave her abuser?" Well, if you have been (or are being) abused, then you know they isolate you from everything and everyone. I felt like I had no way out. I felt hopeless. I felt stuck. I tried to keep going on with my life, but I was still being abused even when I was doing everything he said. From the clothes I wore to the way I styled my hair, everything had to be his way. I got out so many times, but I came back because I thought I couldn't make it. He had taken my joy and my spirit, and I just didn't know what to do. I say, don't be like me. Run. Run as fast as you can. Your abuser can't catch you; you are covered by God.

Don't look back when God gives you a way out. Yes, I hear you saying, "But I don't go to church," or "I don't know God, and I don't know how to pray." Baby, trust me. God hears you. Just have faith and believe. We were all where you are at. I thought I had done so much wrong that God was not going to hear me. I was still married to my kids' father while I was sleeping with my abuser. I didn't feel like I knew how to pray anymore, but I found out that prayer is just communicating with God. If you can talk, do sign language, or send up smoke signals, He will hear you. HALLULEJAH.

Talk to God; I did just that. You can't change your abuser—only God can, and that is only if they want the help. We are not equipped to change anyone. We can only pray for them and let God do the rest.

Sometimes, people and things are removed from our lives so better things can take their place!

Chapter 4

I Totally Understand Your Pain.

I understand everything that you are going through. I've been there. I chose to stay with my abuser, I got married to my abuser even with the abuse because he had more power over me. I even left, but when I came back, it was worse. I was so under his control that I didn't know what to do. I was feeling ashamed and afraid to step out on my own.

I do remember the day when I decided to leave for good. I got help from my daughters, who had never given up on me. One of my daughters called the cops when I needed her the most, and my other daughter opened up her home to me so I could have somewhere to stay when I left my abuser. But, he was telling me that nobody loved me or was going to help me—that he was all I had. I stayed, thinking it was going to get better, but it only got worse.

I remember before I went through an abusive relationship myself, I would see that a woman/man had been abused, and I would always ask the questions, "Why did they stay? Why didn't they just leave?" You just don't know until you have walked a mile in his or her shoes.

I've always seen myself as a strong, independent woman. I knew who I was and knew that I could make it on my own. But when I encountered my abuser, I had just lost everything. My house, my kids, my vehicle, my spiritual walk with Christ, my family, and I almost lost my mind. But like I said before, God wouldn't let that happen to me—He had something for me to do.

My abuser would promise me that he would not hit me anymore. He beat me so badly, but it was always on my body and never my face. He told me, "I will never do it again," and that he was so sorry. I felt like I was in Hell. It was maybe two or three days later that he would do it again.

Mentally, he made me feel like nothing. That is what abusers do; they take your self-esteem, making you feel like nobody wants you so that you feel like you have nowhere to go. You feel like you don't have anyone to turn to because your abuser has isolated you from everyone. I was just so hurt that I didn't know what to do. When I talked on the phone with my mother, or anyone really, he would always make me put it on speaker so that he could hear what they were saying too. This made me feel so helpless, like no one would ever find out what was really going on with me. I felt like I was going to stay stuck in this abusive relationship, and I was very scared

The only thing I had to hold on to was my faith in God. I know now that there had to be somebody praying for me because I remember the day when things started to turn around. God had my abuser make me a prayer room—a room that I could use to pray and pour my soul out to God. I believe God knew that if I stayed any longer, I would not be here today.

The day my abuser went to jail was the best day of my life. I remember going on Facebook and reading this poem by Paulette Kelly, "I got Flowers Today." (You can read this poem at the end of this chapter). This piece really opened my eyes, as I thought about my six kids and what they would do if this man were to kill me. I had to do something, so the next time he hit me, I was able to text my daughter without him knowing and tell her to call the cops. What seemed like a lifetime was about five minutes. I was so nervous, thinking the cops would never get there. He was telling me that I was nothing and that

God was going to punish me. I couldn't believe he thought that what he was doing was right.

He was telling me that he had found another woman and she looked better than me. He was really trying to get my self-esteem to the lowest point that it could go, but all I was thinking was, *"The cops will be here soon, and they are going to take you to jail."*

Finally, I got my freedom. The cops knocked on the door, and I became the best actress in the world. I made myself look surprised that somebody was knocking on my door. We both went to the door, and the cops asked, "Is everything okay in there?" He was blocking the door, but I was behind him, waving my hands, so the cops asked us to step out on the porch. As soon as my feet touched the porch, I felt a rush of freedom. I felt like a little kid again. I pointed to my abuser and said, "He hit me." I felt the childlike faith rush through my body. It was like God had come and rescued me from everything. I knew I was standing in the front yard of my house, but it felt like I was a kid again, playing on the playground, being so free and alive. God had given me childlike faith.

I Got Flowers Today
(Dedicated to Battered Women)

I got flowers today!
It wasn't my birthday or any other special day.
We had our first argument last night;
And he said a lot of cruel things that really hurt;
I know that he is sorry and didn't mean to say the things he said;
Because he sent me flowers today;

I got flowers today.
It wasn't our anniversary or any other special day.
Last night, he threw me into a wall and started to choke me.
It seemed like a nightmare.
I couldn't believe that it was real.
I woke up this morning sore and bruised all over.
I know he must be sorry.
Because he sent me flowers today.

I got flowers today!
And it wasn't Valentine's Day or any other special day;
Last night he beat me and threatened to kill me;
Make-up and long sleeves didn't hide the cuts and bruises this time;
I couldn't go to work today because I didn't want anyone to
know-but I know
He's sorry;
Because he sent me flowers today.

I got flowers today!
And it wasn't Mother's Day or any other special day;
Last night he beat me again, and it was worse than all of the
other times;

I Totally Understand Your Pain.

If I leave him, what will I do? How will I take care of the kids?
What about
Money?
I'm afraid of him, but I'm too scared and dependent to leave
him! But he
Must be sorry;
Because he sent me flowers today.

I got flowers today...
Today was a special day—it was the day of my funeral;
Last night he killed me;
If only I would have gathered the courage and strength to leave him;
I could have received help from the Women's Shelter, but I
didn't ask for
Their help;
So, I got flowers today—for the last time.

By Paulette Kelly
Copyright 1992 Paulette Kelly
All Rights Reserved
www.ardfky.org/sites/ardfky.org/files

"Free at last, Free at last, Thank God almighty I am free at last."
Dr. Martin L. King

Chapter 5

Feeling Alone:
Don't Be Afraid to Ask for Help

After , the police came and took him away, I had to go down to the police department and fill out paperwork. I felt so alone but free. My daughter called me to see if I was okay. She was there from then on making sure I was okay. She went with me to the doctor the next day to see if I had an concussion or not. It turned out that I had a concussion plus a small fracture in my spine. I was able to get in an abuse counselling program, they helped me a lot, but I still felt alone.

Now that you are free and safe and everything has calmed down, now what do you do? I was not afraid to ask for help. I thought my abuser had taken everybody away from me, but that was not the case. I had this wonder couple help me out, and I got my own place. I felt lonely, but everything was going well. I was employee of the month at my job. I looked better because I could now dress how I wanted to dress and wear my hair the way I wanted to.

My self-esteem was building back up. Everything that my abuser took from me, God was giving back to me. But at night when it was just me, I felt lonely. I just didn't know what to do. I started going to church more. I kept the communication with God open even when I felt like nothing was going right. I prayed and talked to God about it.

I was so very tempted to get into another relationship because I couldn't bear the loneliness, but thank God for the people around me that prayed for me and helped me when I was so weak. I had to realize that I had to be healed from the hurt and the pain of being abused. If you don't take anything else from what I have said, take this: After leaving your abuser, don't go back, and don't jump into another relationship so fast. You will hurt that person mentally. You are not healed yourself, and you will feel the same way that you did in the abusive relationship. You will not trust the other person, and there's a chance you could have PTSD (post-traumatic stress disorder).

Once you are out of bondage, don't go back like the Children of Israel, trying to go back to Egypt, back into slavery. I know when you are feeling lonely, you are very tempted to go back. Don't fall for it—just listen to God. Don't trust yourself right now because you are still hurting. You must trust what *God* is saying. Proverbs 3:5-6 (KJV) says, "Trust in the Lord with all thine heart; and lean not unto thine own understanding. In all thy ways acknowledge him, and he shall direct thy paths."

I tried to fight things on my own. I was praying to God every day and going to church, and though I was talking to God, I wasn't completely listening to God. God never said it was going to be easy. It may seem harder now that you are on your own, but you must remember, if you put your faith in God, it will work out. You must wait patiently on the Lord. Psalms 40:1 (KJV) reads, "I waited patiently for the Lord; and he inclined unto me and heard my cry."

I had many people come into my life after I left my abuser, but I would always wonder, "Why are you here? Are you here because you see me as weak and want to cover me by protecting me from the feelings that I have after the abusive relationship and helping me get the help I need? Or do you see me as weak and want to prey on me?" Some people are there for a reason, some are there for season, and some are sent there by God. You must surround yourself with people who love God and not people who just *say* they love God.

You would think that after all that, I would know not to go back to him, but like I said before, I was lonely and didn't know what to do. I was praying but not listening to God. I felt like I was on a merry-go-round, and I just didn't know how to get off. I went back to him again, and the cycle began all over again.

This time, he was mad because I called the police on him, and he said I would not do that again. I was so afraid that I had no choice but to fight back because I didn't want him to kill me. I was in my car, trying to drive away, and he put his hand in the window. I rolled the window up on him and started to drive away. I was blowing my horn and driving so the neighbors would come outside. One neighbor came out. He was a paramedic, and he was about to get the cops there quicker, but my abuser had walked away. I went to my house, got some clothes, left some of my stuff there, and left. He was arrested again, but he didn't stay in long because I didn't press any charges.

I was so messed up inside until I went to therapy. I went to therapy for a while. I had to wait a whole year to divorce my abuser because the law in Fayetteville, North Carolina, was you couldn't divorce your spouse until a year had passed. He kept showing up to my job after he got out of jail. I had to get help from the courts and get a restraining order against him. He even found out where I was living and showed up there. I had roommates though, so he didn't try anything. He would just try to talk me into coming back with him.

I cried myself to sleep at night, thinking about him. I didn't feel the joy that I once had before I met him. God was telling me that just because you have sadness at night doesn't mean there won't come a day when you have joy again. Psalms 30:5 (KJV) reads, "For his anger endureth but a moment, in his favor is life: weeping may endure for a night, but joy cometh in the morning." I was going to church and still felt lonely. I was going to work and still felt lonely. God never said this was going to be easy and there was not going to be trouble in this life.

God said in Psalms 23:4 (KJV), "Yea, though I walk through the valley of the shadow of death, I will fear no evil: for thou art with me;

thy rod and thy staff they comfort me." God wanted to comfort me. Yes, I know the way you are feeling. It seems like God is so far away. I was still feeling alone. I was going on what I thought was best and not what God was telling me: You may feel like you are alone, but you are not alone. God said He will never leave you. It may feel like all hope is lost, but in Matthew 28:20b (KJV), it says, "... and, lo, I am with you always, even unto the end of the world."

I was so very tempted to go back with him. He would come with flowers and other goodies at my job. I was even thinking, *"Maybe he has changed."* But if I didn't do what he told me to do while he was visiting at my job, I could see the change in his face. I knew then that he was still the same person, and I knew I had to go into hiding. I was so glad that the place I stayed in was wonderful. It helped me get my life back, and I felt like I could do a little more for myself and not depend on a man. I finally got my divorce I got the courts to serve him the paperwork to show up to court for the divorce. He didn't show up so I was free once again. The judge gave me the papers and I told him I just want to go back to my God given name "Johnson".

In this season of your life, you must stand up and tell the Devil, *"NO!"* The Devil only comes to take away from you and get you to deny everything God wants you to know. John 10:10a (KJV) reads, "The thief cometh not, but for to steal, and to kill, and to destroy." Jesus is the total opposite of what the Devil is. John 10:10b-11 (KJV) says, "I am come that they might have life, and that they might have it more abundantly. I am the good shepherd: the good shepherd giveth his life for the sheep."

"If tonight you feel alone, wondering,
if anywhere anyone could possibly
be missing you, just know that if they do not miss you,
it is because they do not know you and have not seen
the incredible beauty inside of you."
By Michael Prihoda

Chapter 6

God Gave Me a Voice: This Is My Season

I was so glad that I let God lead me through this season of my life. God helped me as I was getting the help and getting healed. I was on the verge of being completely free, going out, talking to people, and being the person God made me to be. I was healing in the journey. I made new friends; people who came in my life to pray for me, not to prey on me.

I realize God was not pushing me; He was preparing me. I had to trust His plan and not my pain. I put my trust and faith back into God, and He heard me through all the pain and disappointment. God wanted to get me to the place behind the veil where it was just me and God. There, He can take away the hurt and disappointments. The pain of being in an abusive relationship will not hurt anymore if you don't believe it will hurt you.

God asked me the question, *"Can you love passed the pain?"* When I thought about it, I was sure God was asking if I could love another man and be in a healthy relationship again. I met a wonderful man later and got back into church. I was able to love again, but I was still dealing with some hurt and pain.

Remember when I said to not get into a relationship too quickly because you will hurt both yourself and the other person? I had to really focus on God and realize that God was not asking if I could love another man again, but rather, God was asking if I could love *Him* passed all the pain. He was there all the while. He never let my abuser take my life. God wanted me to cry out to Him and have faith that He had me.

Even though I had gotten into another relationship and married him in 2017. I was still not trusting. I couldn't be alone in a closet or bathroom with my husband because I was not healed of the PTSD from the abusive relationship. But God was there, and He started to mend my broken heart. God allow me to see that my husband was there to protect me and keep me safe and pray for me. He brought my husband and I closer. God knew what I needed, and He sent me someone who loved God and knew what I was going through. The husband God has sent me now, he helps me. Like I said before he pushes me to be better. My husband understands the issues that I go through because of his job and the love God has placed in him for me. Just wait on God to give you what you need. Psalms 37:23-24 (KJV) reads, "The steps of a good man are ordered by the Lord: and he delighteth in his way. Though he falls, he shall not be utterly cast down: for the Lord upholdeth him with his hand."

This is my season to put all my faith and trust in God because He is the Author and Finisher of our faith. Hebrews 12:2 (KJV) tells us, "Looking unto Jesus the author and finisher of our faith, who for the joy that was set before him endured the cross, despising the shame, and is set down at the right hand of the throne of God."

God is all you need if you seek Him. Matthew 6:33 (KJV) reads, "But seek ye first the kingdom of God, and his righteousness; and all these things shall be added unto you." You no longer must worry about the pain and disappointment of being abused when God is in your corner. He never said that the things of life will not come upon you, but know that it will not overtake you. Isaiah 54:17 (KJV) says, "No weapon that is formed against thee shall prosper: and every tongue that shall rise against thee in judgement thou shalt condemn. This is the heritage of the servants of the LORD, and their righteousness is of me, saith the LORD."

Regardless of what you've been told, God doesn't give up on you when you get stuck. You can always begin again. Whoever you are, wherever you are, whatever you have been through, it is never too late. You must take one step at a time. If you are determined to succeed in life, God's grace will enable you to do what may seem impossible to your natural thinking. God has promised to do His part, but you have an important part to play as well. When you think you can't make it without your abuser, God is there; He will never leave you.

Deuteronomy 31:6 (KJV) reads, "Be strong and of good courage, fear not, nor be afraid of them: for the Lord thy God, he it is that doth go with thee; not fail thee, nor forsake thee." You have a choice to stay stuck or believe in God for a new beginning. Seek God's will, listen for God's voice, and obey what God says, and He will help you get unstuck every time.

Lies from the Enemy will keep you stuck in your past. Believing what your abuser has said about you will keep you in that place, and you will remain stagnant. My husband always tells me, "Don't keep getting stuck in your past." The grace of God says, *"It's never too late to begin again."* God isn't angry with you, and He isn't distant from you.

Can you love passed the pain? Yes, you can. You can love God, and He will give you the strength to love others.

Break the cycle of violence by jumping off the merry-go-round. Be strong because God will strengthen you for the journey. Don't worry that you're not strong enough before you begin. It is in the journey that God makes you strong. God will guild you and strengthen you. The key is to wait on God and trust Him. He will never leave you nor forsake you.

Hebrews 13:5 (KJV) says, "Let your conversation be without covetousness; and be content with such things as ye have: for he hath said, I will never leave thee, nor forsake thee."

Be grateful for the journey and welcome the new. Don't walk with your head down because of what has happened to you but walk with your head up because you are fearfully and wonderfully made.

Psalm 139:14 (KJV) reads, "I will praise thee; for I am fearfully and wonderfully made; marvelous are thy works; and that my soul knoweth right well."

There will be good days and bad days. There will be days you feel like you can't make it without your abuser, but you must take your life back one day at a time. Get up, brush yourself off, and keep moving. Get involved with something in church, your community, or maybe get back into a healthy hobby that your abuser made you stop.

Like I said before, don't worry if you feel depressed, like you are not going to make it or you're not strong enough. It is through the journey that God makes you strong.

<blockquote>
God offers grace and mercy in your time of need.
You can come to Him fearlessly and with confidence.
</blockquote>

CPSIA information can be obtained
at www.ICGtesting.com
Printed in the USA
BVHW041550141122
651898BV00007B/23